INSIDER'S GUIDE TO THE BODY

The Skeletal System

Laura Gilbert

the rosen publishing group's
rosen
central

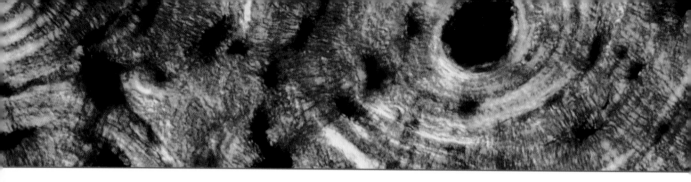

Published in 2001 by The Rosen Publishing Group, Inc.
29 East 21st Street, New York, NY 10010

First Edition

Library of Congress Cataloging-in-Publication Data

Laura Gilbert, 1976–
    The skeletal system / by Laura Gilbert. — 1st ed.
      p. cm. —(The insider's guides to the body)
Includes bibliographical references and index.
    ISBN 0-8239-3338-5 (lib. bdg. : alk. paper)
  1. Human skeleton—Juvenile literature. [1. Skeleton. 2. Bones.]
I. Title. II. Series.
    QM101 .G553 2000
    611'.71—dc21
                          00-010218

Manufactured in the United States of America

Contents

1

The Skeletal System: Framework for the Body

The skeletal system consists of the hundreds of bones that make up the skeleton. In addition to being the framework upon which the human body is built, the skeleton serves many other important purposes.

What Purposes Do Bones Serve?

- PROTECTION

Bones act like the security system for some of the body's most important organs. For example, the skull keeps the brain safe and the ribs protect the lungs.

- RIGIDITY

Bones are the rigid structure of our bodies. They determine the specific size and shape of each of the body's parts.

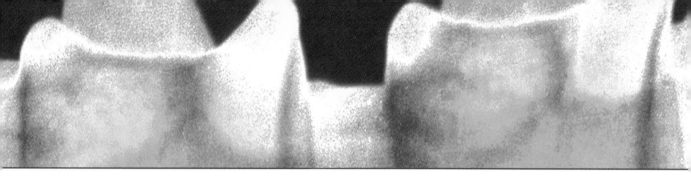

- ## MOVEMENT

  Bones, working together with the muscular system, make it possible for us to move around.

- ## BLOOD CELL MANUFACTURE

  Deep inside some of your bones, a substance called bone marrow produces red blood cells, which help your blood deliver oxygen throughout the body, and white blood cells, which defend the body against illness.

- ## MINERAL STORAGE

  Bones are made up primarily of calcium and phosphorus. If your body requires more of these minerals than is present in the food you have eaten, it can use the reserves stored in your bones.

What's in a Bone?

When you see a skeleton, the bones look like just a bunch of hard, dead objects that give the body shape. But on the inside, bones are packed with living cells and blood.

The outside of a bone, called the periosteum, is very smooth and hard and

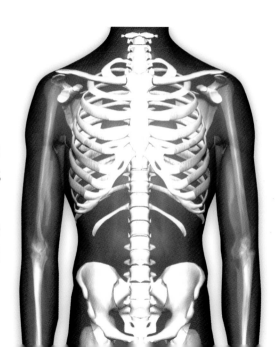

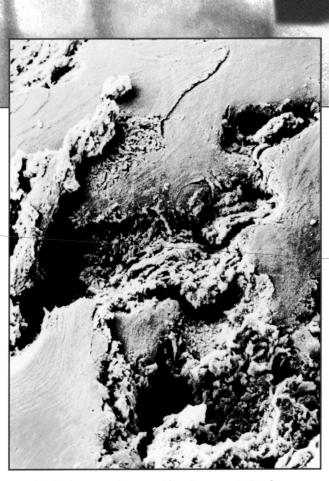

This image (magnification: x55) shows damage done to the surface of a thighbone, or femur, by rheumatoid arthritis. The cartilage that covers the head of the bone is severely eaten away.

is made mostly of calcium. This layer grows over and covers any breaks or cracks in the surface.

Beneath the periosteum is porous bone that is hard but designed to be somewhat lighter. The cells in this area are crisscrossed, which provides lots of support but allows the bone to be lighter than if it were solid. This layer is very thick in the center of many large bones, such as the thighbone, or femur, and thus helps to absorb the impact of movement. This bone matter is made of collagen, a flexible but strong protein, and minerals, mostly calcium and phosphorus, that make the bones hard.

The innermost part of most bones is made up of blood-rich, spongy bone matter filled with soft, fatty tissue called bone marrow.

Types of Bones

Just as there are various purposes for bones, there are also various types of bones.

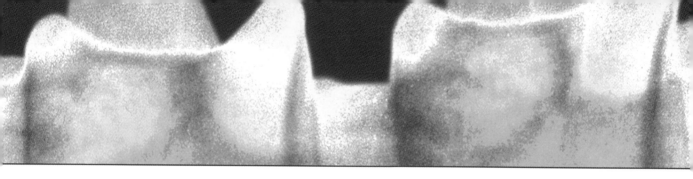

• Long bones are found in the arms and legs. These bones usually have a straight, long shaft with knobby ends. In growing children and teens, the knob is actually slightly separated from the rest of the bone. Once the bone has finished growing, the periosteum will spread over the area to create a smooth surface.

• Short bones are found in the fingers and toes. They allow for precise movements.

• Flat bones are typically thin and flat, and serve to protect the organ they surround. Two good examples are the skull, which protects the brain, and the ribs, which protect, among other things, your heart and your lungs.

• Sesamoid bones serve as accessories to other bones nearby. An example is the kneecap, which works to connect the bones of the upper and lower leg.

• Irregular bones are unique in shape. Their structure is directly related to their job in the body. The vertebrae in the back are good examples of irregular bones.

The Two Skeletons

What would you think if someone told you that you have two skeletons inside you at this very minute? Would you believe the person? Well, in a way, it's true. The skeletal system is divided into two separate

sections. The axial skeleton consists of over 80 bones, including the skull, ribs, and spine. This part of the skeleton protects your brain, spinal cord, and heart, and gives your torso the flexibility to move and twist. The appendicular skeleton consists of over 120 bones that make up the arms, legs, and pelvis. This system provides the framework for your limbs and supports the body's movement.

How Many Bones?

There are probably between 200 and 300 bones in the human body. Why is this number so rough? When a baby is born, he or she has over 300 bones, many of which are made of soft cartilage. A good example is the skull, which, in infants, is made up of various plates. These plates have spaces

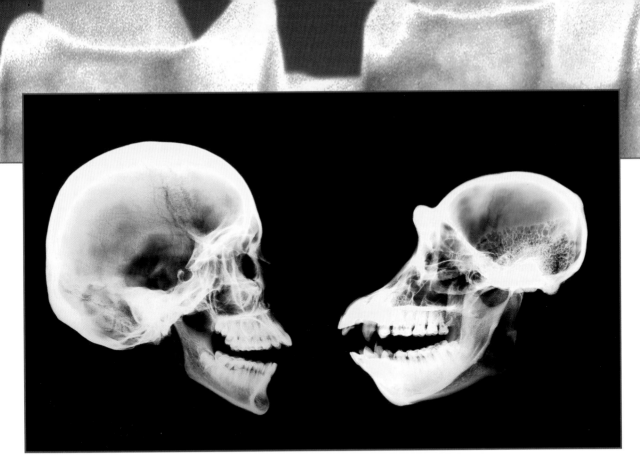

The same bones can be different sizes in different animals. A chimpanzee's skull (right), or cranium, is smaller than a human skull (left), but its jawbone is much larger.

between them so that the baby's head can be squeezed as the child is pushed out of the mother's body. This process creates areas called "soft spots" on a baby's head. By the time the child is one year old, the plates are usually fully fused together. As the child grows, other areas of cartilage turn into bone, and other bones fuse together. As a result, most adults wind up with 206 bones.

A Nose by Any Other Name . . .

Quick—where's your skull? Right. Now—where's your cranium? Actually, that's a trick question. Your skull and your cranium are the same thing. Bones all have their technical names, but they also have common names. To make things even more complicated, some groups of

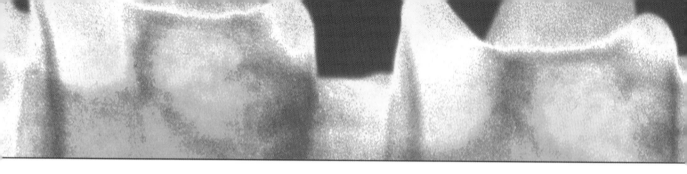

SKELETONS ON PARADE

In the United States, skeletons, like goblins, witches, and ghouls, are a long-standing Halloween costume favorite. In Mexico, the day after Halloween is known as *Dia de los Muertos,* or Day of the Dead. On this special holiday, which commemorates dead loved ones, the departed are often symbolized by tiny detailed skeleton figurines that depict the person's line of work or hobbies.

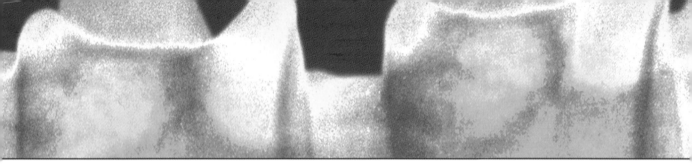

bones have one name that describes the whole group. For example, the ilium, ischium, and pubis bones are commonly referred to by just one name: the pelvis.

Record Breakers

Ever wonder how large your bones can grow, or just how tiny they can be? Here are some answers.

Smallest

The smallest bone in your body can be found inside your ear. It's called the stirrup, and it measures just two millimeters.

Largest

The longest and strongest bone in your body is called the femur—it is your thigh bone. In fully grown humans, this bone accounts for about one-fourth of the person's total height. This means that a six-foot-tall man would have a femur of about one foot, six inches. Check out how long the femur usually grows in other animals.

● Giraffe	1 foot, 9 inches
● Horse	1 foot, 6 inches
● Cat	5 inches
● Rabbit	3 inches

2
How Bones Work

Working Parts: Head to Toe

How are the bones in the body organized? What are the different groups of bones that make up the skeletal system?

Head First!

The human head is made up of twenty-two bones: eight in the cranium and fourteen in the face.

The shape of the skull determines how the face looks: high cheekbones or a rounded face, a wide nose or a long Roman one, a small smile or a broad grin. There are also air-filled tunnels in your skull called sinuses, which connect the nasal cavity and are filled with mucus.

Back Up

When many people hear the term "spinal cord," they think of their backbone, or spine. But, in fact, the spine is only the outer armor of the spinal cord, which is a thick column of nerves that transmits messages from the brain to the rest of the body and back.

The spine is actually made up of several small bones in a row that protect the spinal cord and allow it to move. The seven vertebrae directly under the skull are called the cervical, or neck, bones. The next twelve are referred to as thoracic vertebrae, and the five bones of the lower back are known as lumbar vertebrae.

There are also five sacral bones underneath the lumbar vertebrae, which are fused together into one unmoving part, and four fused bones in the coccyx, or tailbone. Between each bone is a pad of cartilage called a disk, which absorbs shock and keeps the bones from rubbing against one another. Spinal injuries are considered among the most dangerous, since any damage to a vertebra means that the spinal cord inside could be punctured or cut. If this happens, the flow

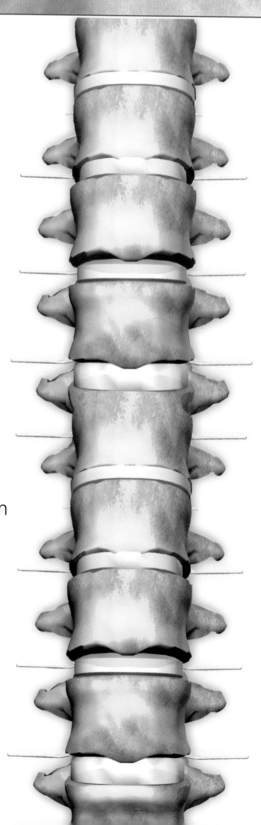

of information between the brain and body parts may stop, often causing paralysis.

Just Ribbing You

In total, humans have twelve pairs of long, flat bones called the ribs. The seven uppermost pairs are attached to the sternum, or breastbone, by cartilage. The three pairs below this section (the eighth, ninth, and tenth pairs) are not attached directly to the sternum, but rather to the seventh pair of ribs. The eleventh and twelfth pairs are not attached to anything in the front of the body and thus are known as "floating" ribs.

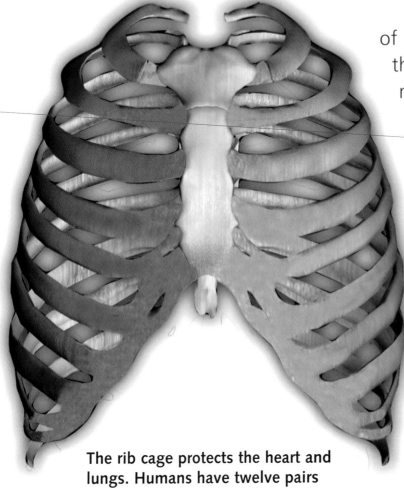

The rib cage protects the heart and lungs. Humans have twelve pairs of ribs.

Ribs protect the heart and lungs and aid in breathing by expanding to let the lungs take in oxygen and moving in a downward motion to help with exhalation (breathing out).

Shoulders to Tail

The bones running from your collarbone to your shoulders give your upper body its shape and provide anchors for the arm bones at the shoulder. The pelvis provides a similar service for the lower body. The body's largest bone, the femur (thighbone), fits in the lower pelvis. The pelvis is also specially shaped to protect your intestines and reproductive organs. The female's pelvis is larger than a male's, which allows her to carry and deliver children.

Arms and Legs

Your extremities, or arms and legs, are attached by joints to the main part of your skeleton. Your arms are lighter and less powerful than your legs, which makes it easier for your lower body to bear the weight of the upper body. Both your arms and legs consist of a strong upper bone—the femur (thigh) in the leg and the humerus (upper arm) in the arm. There are also two thinner bones in the lower portion—the tibia and fibula in the shin, and the radius and ulna in the forearm.

A series of sliding joints and a series of short bones called metacarpals (in the hand) and metatarsals (in the foot) let

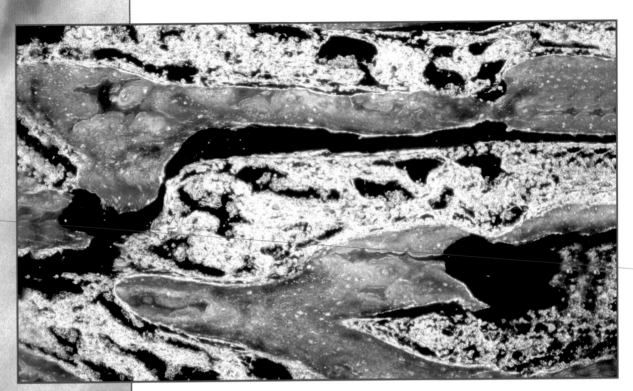

In some parts of the body, cartilage gradually turns into bone as a person develops. The image above (magnification: x33) shows calcified cartilage.

the hands and feet move around with ease. At the very tip are bones called phalanges, but we know them better as fingers and toes. The bones in your hands are some of the smallest and most precise in the body. There are twenty-nine bones in the hand alone, some of which are attached to muscles that run all the way up the forearm.

Moving Parts

All of these bones don't do much good on their own. However, when they're surrounded by and connected to other tissues, the bones allow us to move. The place where two or more bones meet is called a joint.

Joint Tissue

There are three types of tissue commonly found at joints.

● Cartilage is soft and flexible, but sturdy. It is found between bones, where it works to absorb shock. Fibrous cartilage between bones is called menisci. Cartilage is also found in some body parts, such as your ears and nose.

In some parts of the body, such as the skull, cartilage slowly turns into bone as a person develops.

● A tendon connects muscle to bone. Movement happens when the muscle, which is attached to a bone with a tendon, contracts. It is the skeletal muscles of the muscular system that contract and pull our bones back and forth.

● Ligaments are tough, fibrous tissue that connect one bone to another. Instead of helping you move, like tendons, ligaments keep the bones aligned properly. For example, there are four tendons in each of your knees. They keep your kneecap and leg bones in place when your knee bends.

Bones and cartilage are surrounded by a slippery substance known as synovial fluid. This fluid fills the empty spaces between joints and ensures that bones can move smoothly. Think of it as your body's own motor oil.

Types of Joints

A joint is the place where any two bones meet and join together. There are several kinds of joints in the body, each of which allows for a specific type of movement. For example, you can move your ankle in a complete circle, but not your knee. Below is a list of the most common types of joints in the body.

Immovable Joints

Two bones that are connected by only a thin layer of tissue or that can't move independently are connected with an immovable, or fixed, joint. The different bones in the skull are connected with immovable joints, as are many of the bones in the lower part of your spine.

Hinge Joints

Hinge joints are usually what come to mind when people think of joints. Some examples are the knuckles, elbows, and knees. A hinge joint consists of two or more bones meeting at one point. It allows for back-and-forth motion, like a door.

Ball-and-Socket Joints

This type of joint is made up of a long bone with a knob at the end, the ball, that sits in a rounded cavity, the socket, of another bone. The joint where the upper arm connects to the shoulder, and the femur to the pelvis, creates a ball-and-socket joint, which allows for swinging motions. A joystick is one example of a ball-and-socket joint with which video game players may be familiar.

Pivot Joints

A pivot joint consists of one bone stacked on top of another and allows for pivoting, or twisting, movements.

Gliding Joints

Gliding joints are made up of small bones connected by a web of tendons and ligaments. These joints can move in innumerable directions—back and forth, side to side, around, in any combination. The ankles and wrists are made of gliding joints.

Saddle Joints

This unique type of joint, called the saddle

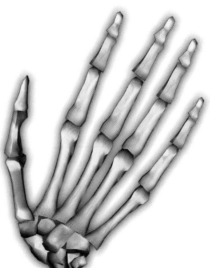

At a hinge joint, two or more bones meet at one point, allowing for back-and-forth movement. Your knuckles are examples of hinge joints.

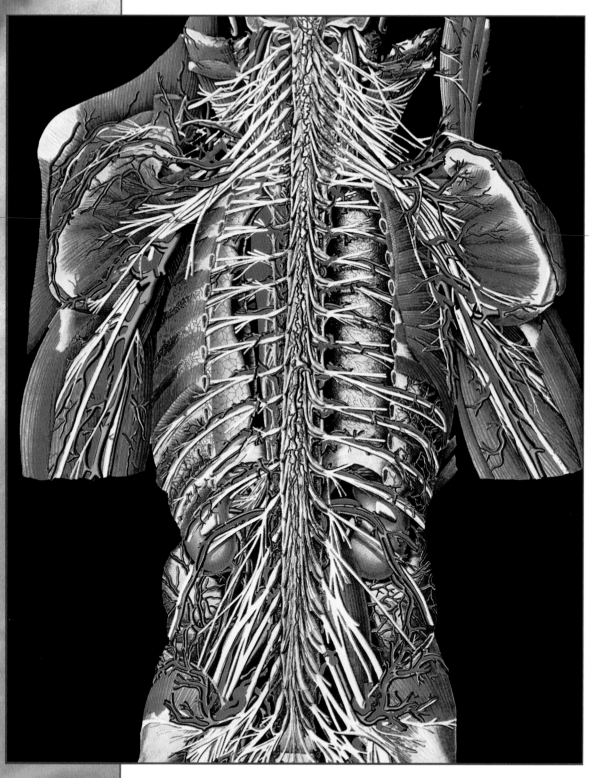

The spine is made up of small bones called vertebrae. This structure protects the spinal cord, while allowing the back to move freely.

because of its shape, allows the thumb to move sideways across the palm.

How Does the Spine Work?

The spine, or backbone, is made up of small bones called vertebrae. It supports your body, allowing you to stand up straight, and surrounds and protects the spinal column. To understand how this works, imagine one of those jump ropes that is made of plastic segments. The rope underneath represents your spinal cord, which is flexible but not sturdy. The plastic pieces are like the individual vertebrae.

Having the spine composed of hard bone, but divided into many pieces, allows it to move freely while keeping the spinal cord well protected.

What Is Double-Jointedness?

You may have heard someone say that he or she is "double-jointed," or can move a joint in the opposite way that it's supposed to move. No one actually has two joints in one place, but some people naturally do have longer-than-normal ligaments. Imagine a ligament as a string holding two bones together. In double-jointed people, the ligament is more like a rubber band, allowing the two bones to be moved farther apart.

3
Keeping Bones Healthy

Your Job

Since bones are made mostly of calcium, the single most important thing you can do for your skeleton is to get plenty of calcium. Unfortunately, most young people today don't get enough. Many of us rely on junk food to get us through the day, which means we consume more soda pop than milk and more prepackaged snacks than green, leafy vegetables.

It is recommended by the United States Food and Drug Administration (FDA) that young people between the ages of nine and eighteen consume 1300 milligrams of calcium each day; adults need 1000 milligrams. The reason that young people need more is simple: Their bones are still growing.

Got Milk?

One of the best sources of calcium is milk. A single eight-ounce glass of milk—skim, whole, or low fat—contains 300 milligrams (mg) of calcium. Yogurt is another food that is high in calcium, and cheese contains a fair amount as well. You can also either take calcium supplements (or multivitamins with extra calcium) or look for foods that are calcium enriched to make sure you get enough.

But the best way to ensure that you take in enough calcium is to eat a well-balanced diet: turnip greens, tofu, spinach, pudding, and navy beans all have over 100 mg of calcium per cup. Broccoli, almonds, chickpeas, and sweet potatoes have less but are still good sources. But the real calcium superstars, if you can handle the taste, are sardines. They have a whopping 351 mg per can!

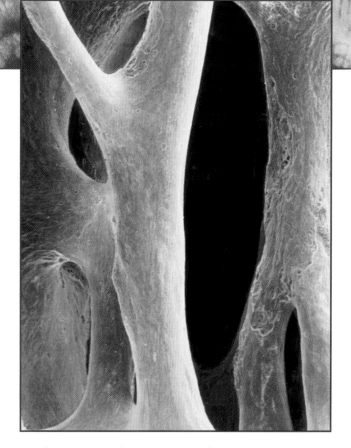

The image above (magnification: x105) is a view of spongy, or cancellous, bone tissue. Because bones are made primarily of calcium, it's important to get enough calcium in your diet.

Maximize Your Intake

There are also ways to maximize your body's calcium consumption. Taking supplements between meals together with a small protein-rich snack will help your body digest the calcium in the supplements. Vitamin D, vitamin K, and magnesium all help the body

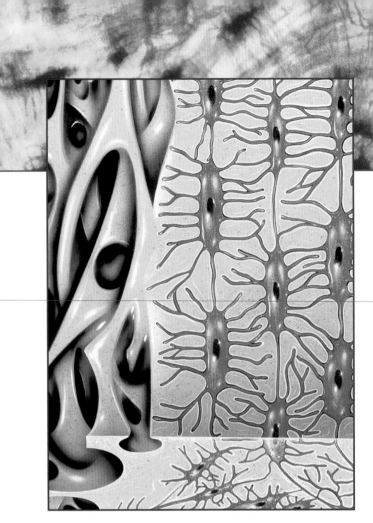

This illustration shows the microstructure of human bone. Weight-bearing exercise stimulates the growth of the cells in your bones, making them stronger.

absorb calcium. On the other hand, too much caffeine, alcohol, and nicotine will do the opposite: These substances actually make it more difficult for your body to absorb calcium.

Certain over-the-counter and prescription drugs can also interfere with calcium absorption. Be sure to talk to your doctor if you take aluminum-based antacids or drugs for asthma, lupus, or arthritis. Other drugs that can inhibit calcium absorption are those used to treat thyroid disorders, high cholesterol, epilepsy, and heart problems.

Exercise

Regular exercise can help keep your bones strong. It may seem like the opposite should be true—that running and jumping would wear your bones down. But the truth is that every time you take a step, lift a weight, dance to your favorite song, or go for a run, you put pressure on your bones. This is called weight-bearing exercise. (Swimming and yoga are examples of exercises that are good for you, but they are not weight-bearing.)

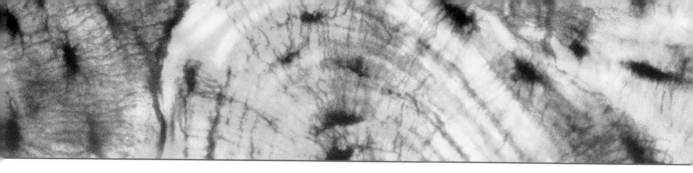

Weight-bearing exercise stimulates the cells in your bones to make them stronger. This means that you will have a harder, tougher skeleton when you're older, which will help prevent pain and breaks.

People Who Care About Your Bones

There is a whole range of experts who treat problems related to the skeletal system, drawing on information and techniques from many different disciplines.

General Practitioner

This is the person you probably refer to as your family doctor—a medical doctor who can treat a variety of physical problems. A general practitioner is probably your first stop for basic aches and pains that may be related to your bones.

Orthopedic Surgeon

An orthopedic surgeon is a specialist—a type of doctor with particular expertise—in bone problems. An orthopedic surgeon treats a variety of serious bone disorders and broken bones.

Doctors of Osteopathy

Doctors of osteopathy are medically trained specialists, similar to but not MDs, with a more holistic—or whole-body—approach. The fundamental idea behind osteopathy is that imbalances of mus-

More Jobs with Skeletons

When you think of someone who specializes in bones, you probably imagine a doctor in the ER, not in the FBI. But there's a special field of detective work that uses clues found from the skeleton to help identify crime victims and gain information.

These detectives are called forensic anthropologists, and they use their knowledge of physical anthropology—the study of the changes in human bones based on life and environment—to help piece together crime scenes. A forensic anthropologist is often called in when a skeleton is found with no clues about its identity or how the person died.

By studying the skeleton, or even just parts of it, the scientist can often deduce some of the following information:

● Height: Measuring certain bones can tell the anthropologist how tall the person probably stood.

● Sex: The bones of men and women are slightly different. A trained anthropologist can tell them apart. By looking at the pelvis, an anthropologist can even figure out whether a woman had children.

● Age: As a person ages, his or her bones go through various changes. For example, very young children often have cartilage instead of fully developed wrist bones; growing teens have long bones with separated knobby ends; the pubic bones in adults have bumps and ridges that gradually smooth over; and older people may have visible arthritic conditions.

● Weight: Ligaments leave marks where the bone attaches to muscle. If a person is very strong, the marks will be bigger, indicating how much muscle mass, and thus bulk, a person carried.

● Injuries: Marks on the skeleton can often reveal whether a person was stabbed, shot, burned, or beaten and even predict whether the injury was fatal.

● DNA: Bones and tooth pulp can all contain DNA, a person's individual genetic code. If compared to DNA samples found from a missing person's hair, saliva, or skin, scientists can tell whether they belong to the same person.

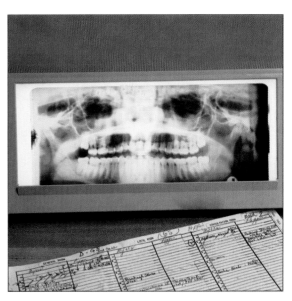

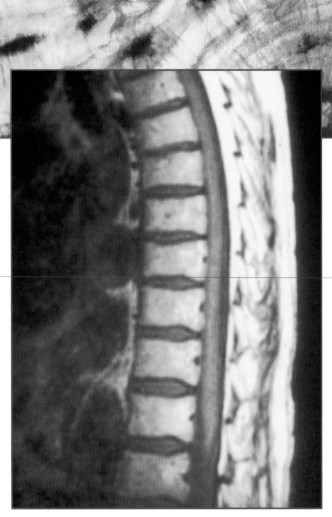

Chiropractors believe that many health problems stem from misalignment of the vertebrae.

cles, bones, ligaments, and tissues are often the root of problems, and that proper realignment may stimulate the body to self-heal. Treatments can include massage, stretching, physical therapy, or gentle touching. A subsection of osteopathy, called cranial osteopathy, uses a light touch on the bones of the skull to heal problems.

Chiropractors

Chiropractors believe that many problems—from allergies to arthritis—stem from the bones in the back, the vertebrae, being misaligned, or off-kilter. The theory is that when the bones aren't lined up, nerve function is disrupted. Chiropractors apply pressure to your limbs and back in an effort to move the vertebrae back into their proper position.

There is, however, a lot of controversy in the medical community about whether or not chiropractic treatments actually work. Some even claim that chiropractic treatments may be harmful and lead to injuries. If you have an interest in being treated by a chiropractor, ask him or her, or a trusted doctor, about any risks you may face.

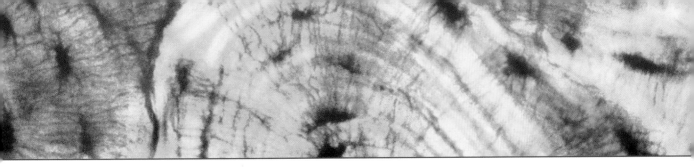

Doctor Detectives

When you go to the doctor for a problem that you think may involve your bones, he or she has to rely on your reports to decide what's wrong. Since the doctor can't always see what is going wrong, he or she has to use your description of the pain to decide what the next step should be. Doctors are specially trained to look beyond your basic complaint that "it hurts" to figure out what's really wrong. Here are some ways that a doctor can diagnose your hidden problem.

● **Your Face:** If your arm hurts, why would the doctor look at your face? He or she wants to see how your expression changes when certain body parts are touched or moved. Many people are shy or nervous around doctors and don't want to speak up while the doctor is doing an examination, so nonverbal clues are important ways for a doctor to figure out what body part is causing the problem.

● **How You Stand and Walk:** If you're suffering from back pain and a doctor notices that you are limping, he or she may guess that the problem stems from overstraining half of your back. Your posture and gait can give the doctor an idea of whether there is an underlying problem that is causing the pain that is bothering you.

● **Your Job and Hobbies:** A person's particular line of work and what he or she does for fun can definitely contribute to specific health problems. For example, a softball player's sore shoulder may be attributed to his or her constant throwing, while a waiter's back pain could be caused by carrying around heavy trays. So if your doctor asks what sports you play or what hand you write with, he or she may be making more than small talk. Answering the doctor in detail may actually tell him or her what is causing the problem.

● **How You Describe the Pain:** Just because the doctor has a medical degree doesn't mean that he or she is the only expert in the room. You are the only person who can explain exactly where the pain is and how it is affecting you. The more detail you give, the more likely it is that the doctor will be able to narrow down the cause of your problem. "My knee hurts" can mean many things. But saying, "My knee starts to hurt toward the end of workouts. It's a sharp pain right below my kneecap that lasts for a couple of hours afterward" tells the doctor that your problem is very different from the problem of someone who says, "I get a dull pain in the back of my knee whenever I walk."

Look Inside Yourself

The most common way for doctors to look at your bones is by using an X-ray machine. The machine sends a certain frequency of light ray

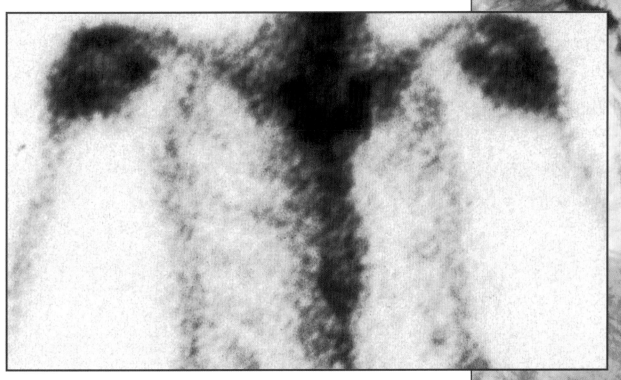

X-ray machines enable a doctor to examine the bones inside a patient's body.

through your body to be photographed on X-ray film. The light can pass through solid matter with a low density—such as your skin and organs—but not high density, like your bones. That's why your bones show up on an X ray. The doctor can take a detailed look at the bones and see whether, where, and how they are broken without having to operate.

An arthroscope is also used to examine patients' joints or knees. This instrument allows doctors to view various details and angles of body parts without having to perform an operation.

4

Bone Injuries, Diseases, and Disorders

Occasionally, accidents get the better of our flexible, strong bones, and they do break. There are three ways to describe an injury that involves a broken bone: closed, where only the bone is affected; open, where the bone has poked through the skin or is exposed to the air through the skin; and compound, where other structures near the bone, such as nerves or arteries, are affected by the injury.

Types of Fractures

There are further ways to describe the fracture in the bone itself.

● Stress fractures are minor cracks on the bone's surface that are caused by overuse.

● Linear means that the break involves a single line across the bone and may be in a diagonal pattern.

● Spiral refers to the spiral pattern around the bone, caused when a bone is twisted to the point of snapping.

- Commuted is another word for crushed. The bone has been broken into several smaller pieces.

- Transverse means the break runs directly across the bone.

- Greenstick fractures refer to a bone that has split on one side but remains whole on the other. You can see this kind of break illustrated by bending a freshly cut stick to one side until it starts to break on one side—that is what a greenstick fracture looks like.

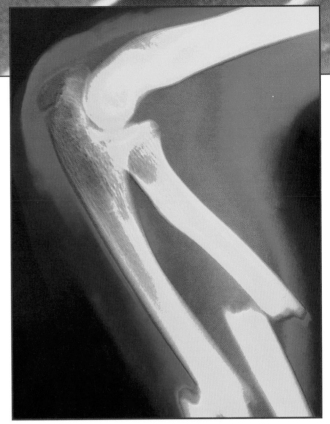

This is a compound fracture of the forearm. Once they are reset, fractured bones can heal themselves and grow back together.

How Do Bones Heal?

One amazing thing about bones is that they are designed to heal themselves. First, a doctor resets the bone, or fits the broken pieces back together. Once it has been reset, a broken or fractured bone will start to reknit its cells and become whole again. The top layer usually grows over the break first, smoothing out the seams, and is followed by the tough, bony matter underneath.

Protecting the Injury

There are several ways to keep the pieces of bone still enough so that the bone can mend itself without being knocked out of place.

Casts

You have no doubt seen these hard, white bandages on the arms or legs of friends who have broken bones. Casts are usually used on limbs when there's a simple fracture that will easily heal if it is just kept still. The cast keeps the body part absolutely still, while adding enough weight to stimulate bone cell regrowth.

Cast Braces

This is a cast that is usually used for breaks in the leg that will heal properly even when the knee is allowed to move a little. It comes in two parts—one piece for above the knee and one for below. Before the plaster dries, a flexible joint is placed between the sections so that the patient can bend his or her knee.

Traction

If a bone breaks and isn't used again, often it will never heal. Bones need constant pressure and use in order to signal the body to regenerate. If a patient is forced to be bedridden after an injury, frequently he or she will be put in traction. In this technique, a plaster cast is attached to a pulley system that exerts steady force on the break, stimulating the bone to mend itself.

External Fixation

This type of setting requires pins to be run through the bone parts, then stuck to a thin metal piece that remains outside the body. Doctors have to use an external fixation when the break will not heal properly just by keeping the area still, such as with a cast.

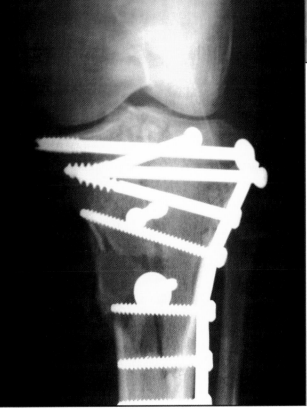

In one form of internal fixation, a metal plate is attached to the outside of a bone with screws drilled through the broken pieces to keep them in place.

Internal Fixation

There are several types of bone repair that must be done inside the body. Sometimes doctors insert long screws through parts of bone, securing bones to one another. In another configuration, a metal plate is attached to the outside of the bone, with screws drilled through the broken pieces and attached to the plate, to keep the bone in the right formation as it heals. Other times doctors stick a long metal rod down the center of a long broken bone, then screw the broken pieces of bone to the pin in the center. Often once the bone is healed, the pins stay inside the patient.

Internal fixation is used when a bone is crushed into many pieces or the break is so severe that external fixation is not sufficient enough to keep everything aligned so that it will heal properly.

And Finally . . . Superglue?

Superglue works on almost anything, right? So why not use it on bones? Actually, doctors in the United States do occasionally use a fast-drying liquid cement to help bind broken bones that might otherwise take weeks to heal on their own.

Sports Injuries

Injuries sustained during athletic activity can happen to people of all ages and fitness levels. Any blow or misstep can result in a sudden problem, and repeated use can wear down body parts and cause pain. When an athlete ignores pain and continues to exercise, he or she runs the risk of injuring the body part even more. Below are a few of the most common problems among athletes.

Shin Splints

This is a common complaint of runners and usually occurs when a person first begins exercising or starts running on hard surfaces. Each time the foot hits the ground, the arch flattens, pulling the muscles that are attached to that part of the foot downward. This constant tugging causes a lingering pain in the tendons that attach the muscle to the bones of the shin.

Shoulder Dislocations

This common injury occurs when a person moves his or her arm in a rapid motion and causes the arm bone to be wrenched partially or completely out of the shoulder socket. Basketball, baseball, and football players are just some of the athletes prone to this injury because of the rapid throwing motion they repeatedly practice.

Bone Spurs

Sometimes when the body heals a bone, it deposits extra calcium and minerals in places where the bone didn't originally grow. This can cause a lump in the bone where the break had been.

Other times, a tendon is pulled or a joint is worn down, and the body tries to heal itself by depositing bone material that can cause pain and make movement difficult. In avid runners, this often happens in the foot: The tissue holding up the arch of the foot is constantly under strain, and the body tries to reinforce it by depositing bone where the tissue meets the heel. (This is also a problem obese people face because their weight puts too much pressure on their arches.) This causes what looks like a bump to form on the bone and is referred to as a heel spur.

Other Diseases and Disorders

There are many disorders that can affect the health of your bones. Each bone in each area can have a range of problems. There are

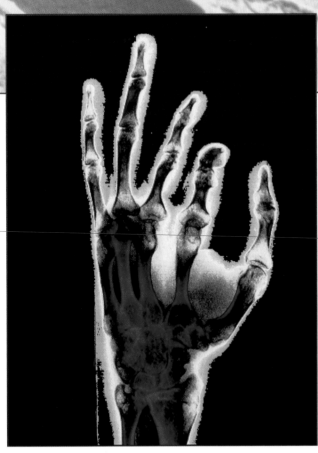

Arthritis is the name given to a number of problems that cause the joints to become inflamed. Above is an X ray of rheumatoid arthritis.

also different types of problems that affect the skeleton: endocrine disorders that alter how bones grow; problems with cartilage, ligaments, and tendons that affect the joints' function; and diseases of the bones themselves. Below are just a few of the most common disorders that affect the skeletal system.

Arthritis

This general term refers to any of a number of problems that cause the joints to become inflamed—disease, infection, aging, even genetic defects. Stiffening and soreness are the most common symptoms of arthritis, which can sometimes be treated with medicine.

Osteoporosis

Osteoporosis, a weakening of the bones, is the most common bone disorder in the United States, affecting 24 million Americans. Eighty percent of sufferers are women, and most are past their forties. In this condition, the bones lose mass, leaving them weak and much more likely to break. Patients with osteoporosis often break their spines, hips, or wrists in falls. Adequate calcium intake and weight-bearing exercise are the best prevention for osteoporosis.

Scoliosis

In some cases, the spine grows in a slight S-curve, which can impede its ability to provide support and flexibility. A brace is often enough to correct the curvature. A related problem called kyphosis refers to the curvature of the upper backbones, resulting in what is referred to as a hunchback.

BONE MARROW TRANSPLANTS

When a person's bone marrow is not working, he or she may need to receive a bone marrow transplant. Marrow is extracted from a healthy individual using a long, strong needle that is inserted into a marrow-producing bone such as the breastbone, pelvis, or leg. The marrow is then injected directly into a vein of the recipient, where it is reabsorbed by the blood.

The blood of the recipient must identically match that of the donor so that the recipient's body accepts the cells as its own. Usually, a close family member donates marrow because finding strangers who match can be very difficult.

Avascular Necrosis

A harsh blow to the knee, hip, or other joint can pinch the veins and nerves in the area, cutting off the joint's blood supply. When that happens, the cartilage and bone stop growing and can even die. Called avascular necrosis, the condition can reach the point where surgery is required.

That's what happened to Bo Jackson, who was forced to retire from football and baseball because of necrosis in his hip—he wound up getting a hip replacement—and Garrison Hearst of the San Francisco 49ers, who has undergone surgery for the condition in his ankle.

Bones for Life

Bones are not hard, inactive supports under your skin. They are alive. They help keep you healthy, make sure that you are able to move around, and keep delicate organs safe. And when accidents do happen, you can be sure that your bones will react to get you back in working order. Keeping your bones in good shape, with proper nutrition and exercise, is a key ingredient to an active and healthy life.

Glossary

appendicular skeleton
Bones of the arms, legs, and pelvis.

arthritis
Any of a number of conditions that cause inflammation of the tissues of the joints.

axial skeleton
Bones of the skull, spine, and ribs.

bone
Hard piece of matter, primarily consisting of calcium and phosphorus, that makes up part of the skeletal system; it gives the body its shape, protects internal organs, and allows for movement.

bone marrow
Spongy material found at the center of some bones that manufactures blood cells.

calcium
Mineral used in the formation of bones; it exists in high amounts in milk and other dairy products.

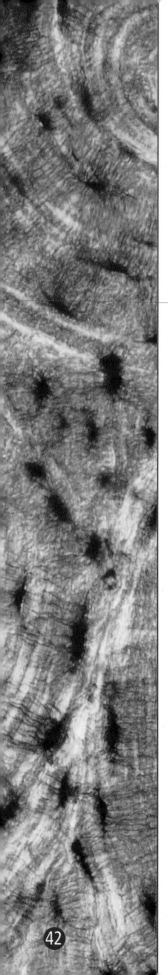

cartilage
A soft, flexible, but sturdy tissue. It is found between bones and in some body parts, such as the ears.

chiropractor
Health practitioner who focuses on realignment of the bones in the back.

cranium
The bones surrounding the brain; also called the skull.

forensic anthropologist
Person who studies bones to aid in police and legal cases.

fracture
A break in a bone.

joint
Place where two or more bones come together; may be hinge, ball-and-socket, pivot, saddle, or fixed.

ligament
Tissue that connects a bone to a bone.

muscle
Contracting fiber that attaches to bone and, when contracted, causes movement.

orthopedics
Field of medicine that focuses on fixing bone disorders and problems.

osteoporosis
Loss of bone mass that results in a weakening of the bone.

skeletal system
Set of bones and connective tissues that make up the body's framework.

spinal cord
Column of nerves that runs up the back and processes messages between the brain and the rest of the body.

sports injury
Pain or other problem caused by physical activity, overuse, or misuse.

traction
Form of treating broken bones that attaches weighted pulleys to casts to add pressure and spur bone growth.

vertebrae
Bones of the back with column in middle through which the spinal cord passes.

weight-bearing exercise
Any physical activity that puts weight on the bones of the body and creates bone mass.

X ray
A method using light waves that pass through skin but not bone, allowing doctors to photograph and examine the bones.

For More Information

In the United States

Centers for Disease Control and Prevention (CDC)
1600 Clifton Road
Atlanta, GA 30333
(404) 639-3534
(800) 311-3435
Web site: http://www.cdc.gov

National Institutes of Health (NIH)
Visitor Information Center
Bethesda, MD 20892
(301) 496-1776
Web site: http://www.nih.gov

World Health Organization (WHO)
Regional Office for the Americas/Pan American Health
    Organization
525 23rd Street NW

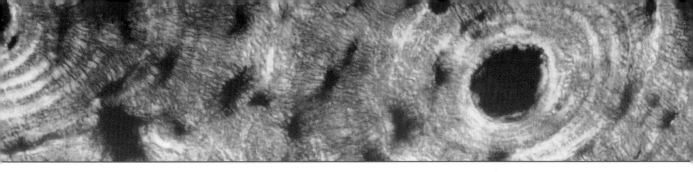

Washington, DC 20037
(202) 974–3000
Web site: http://www.paho.org or
Web site: http://www.who.int

In Canada

Health Canada
A.L. 0913A
Ottowa, ON K1A OK9
(613) 957-2991
Web site: http://www.hc-sc.gc.ca/

Web Sites

General Medical Information
http://www.mayohealth.org
http://www.onhealth.com

KidsHealth
http://www.kidshealth.org
This site provides lots of easy-to-understand information about all
    kinds of medical and health issues.

National Osteoporosis Foundation
http://www.nof.org

Information on Day of the Dead
http://www.olvera-street.com

For Further Reading

Gallavotti, Barbara. *The Human Body in Action.* New York: Barron's Educational Series, 1999.

Jackson, Donna M. *The Bone Detectives*. Boston: Little, Brown & Co., 1996.

Llewellyn, Claire. *The Big Book of Bones: An Introduction to Skeletons.* New York: Peter Bedrick Books, 1998.

Montagu, Ashley. *The Elephant Man: A Study in Human Dignity*. Lafayette, LA: Acadian House Publishing, 1996.

Pressman, Alan H. *The Complete Idiot's Guide to Vitamins and Minerals.* New York: Alpha Books, 1997.

Silverstein, Alvin. *Skeletal System*. New York: Twenty-first Century Books, 1994.

Taylor, Barbara. *Skeleton.* New York: DK Publishing, 1998.

Treays, Rebecca. *Understanding Your Muscles and Bones.* London: Usborne, 1997.

VanCleave, Janice. *Janice VanCleave's The Human Body for Every Kid.* New York: John Wiley & Sons, 1995.

Walker, Richard. *The Visual Dictionary of the Skeleton.* New York: DK Publishing, 1995.

Index

Credits

About the Author

Laura Gilbert is a freelance writer from Brooklyn, New York, and has worked as an editor at *Cosmopolitan* and *Fitness* magazines. Ms. Gilbert also suffered a broken arm, which healed nicely, when she was in fourth grade.

Photo Credits

Pp. 5, 13, 14, 15, 29 © Life Art, p. 6 © Moredun Animal Health Ltd/Science Photo Library (SPL)/Photo Researchers, Inc.; p. 8 © Custom Medical; p. 9 © D. Roberts/SPL/Photo Researchers Inc.; p. 10 Rose Palmisano/The Albuquerque Journal/AP/Worldwide; p. 16 © Mike Peres, RBP/Custom Medical; p. 20 © Mehau Kulyk/Science Photo Library/Photo Researchers Inc.; p. 23 © Prof. P. Motta/Dept. of Anatomy/University "La Sapienza," Rome/SPL/Photo Researchers, Inc.; p. 24 © John Bavosi/SPL/Photo Researchers, Inc.; p. 27 © Blair Seitz/Photo Researchers, Inc.; p. 28 © J. Croyle/Custom Medical; p. 31 © Keith/Custom Medical; p. 33 © Dept. of Clinical Radiology, Salisbury District Hospital/SPL/Photo Researchers, Inc.; p. 35 © Photo Researchers; p. 38 © Michael English, M.D./Custom Medical.

Cover, front matter, and back matter © Michael Abbey/Photo Researchers, Inc.: color enhanced image of Haversian canals of human bone.

Ch. 1 © SPL/Photo Researchers, Inc.: color enhanced X ray of four lumbar vertebrae of human spine.

Ch. 2 © Department of Clinical Radiology, Salisbury District Hospital/SPL/Photo Researchers, Inc.: X ray image of fractured skull.

Ch. 3 © Michael Abbey/Photo Researchers, Inc.: human bone tissue magnified 50x.

Ch. 4 © David Bewsey, Ethicon Ltd. and University of Glasgow/Science Photo Library/Photo Researchers, Inc.: color enhanced image of tendon cells grown by scientists on a "smart bandage," magnified 330x.

Series Design

Cindy Williamson

Layout

Geri Giordano